Harvest

poems by

Britt Allen

Finishing Line Press
Georgetown, Kentucky

Harvest

Copyright © 2021 by Britt Allen
ISBN 978-1-64662-552-9 First Edition
All rights reserved under International and Pan-American Copyright Conventions. No part of this book may be reproduced in any manner whatsoever without written permission from the publisher, except in the case of brief quotations embodied in critical articles and reviews.

ACKNOWLEDGMENTS

I would like to say a big thank you to the following journals for their publication of individual poems:

"Does My Brother Dream of Shower?" in *Sugar House Review*
"Harvest" originally in *Narrative Magazine*
"Mastectomy," "Domesticated," and "January" in *Sink Hollow Literary Magazine*
"Inscape" in *Pink Panther Magazine*

I could not have done the work without the support from my mentor and thesis chair, Professor Shanan Ballam. Thank you for helping me find myself. Thank you also to my committee members, Dr. Ben Gunsberg and Dr. Dennise Gackstetter, for the time and feedback and care.

Thank you to my writing groups, past and present. An especially big thanks to Helicon West, Poetry at Three, and my patron saint, Star Coulbrooke.

Thank you to my boys, Nathan and Burkley, for the big patience and unconditional love.

Publisher: Leah Huete de Maines
Editor: Christen Kincaid
Cover Art: Nathan Allen
Author Photo: Jordan McDonald
Cover Design: Elizabeth Maines McCleavy

Order online: www.finishinglinepress.com
also available on amazon.com

Author inquiries and mail orders:
Finishing Line Press
PO Box 1626
Georgetown, Kentucky 40324
USA

Table of Contents

Harvest 1

Can This Marriage Be Avoided 2

To My Husband 3

Selfish 4

The Goldfish 7

Dissonance 8

Deboned 9

Exposition 10

Transatlantic Relapse 11

Stepfather as Wolf 12

To My Husband 13

Inscape 14

Three Little Sisters 15

To My Husband 16

After Watching the Performance Poem,
    "We Keep Our Victims Ready" 17

Does My Brother Dream of Showers 19

Too awake 20

Domesticated 21

Mastectomy 22

January 23

Alaska 24

Harvest

My family split up in the cornfield.
God knows why. I called my stepfather
Daddy at eleven years old,
paired off with him in the maze.
The sun went down and Daddy stopped
on the muddy path, unzipped his leather jacket, swallowed
me into the mask of brown cologne and stiff animal skin.
His arm bore down the neck of my coat, shirt, wiry
hairs tickling my collarbone and chin, his stone hand reaped my
    chest—
the year's fruit in his palm. He gathered
me to him, his cold erection pawing my spine.
Mom could have been an acre away,
or doe-still behind the next stalk.
My straw body lifted with her husband's groans, fell with his sigh.
Whatever he found reaching for my underwear
almost made him weep.
God knows why.

Can This Marriage Be Avoided?

specimen, but he gave forth an aroma and appearance of masculinity strong enough to charm a Nod maiden out of a tree.

Could a modern man, walking down that forest trail so long ago, have done as well? From her tree the Nod maiden would have beheld a baldheaded, clean-shaven, pot-bellied little squirt wearing plastic-rimmed spectacles, his mouth full of safety pins, a dishtowel draped over one shoulder, a diaper in his hand, and muscles so poorly developed he would have to tip the bellboy to get assistance carrying his bride over the threshold of his honeymoon hotel. The maiden would probably have fallen out of her tree all right, but it would have been because of laughter rather than any irresistible urge to mate with such a creature. The power of women accomplished this horrendous transformation; when the descendants of the Nod maidens started to civilize the male, they succeeded in damn near wrecking him.

It was ordained that man, in his gestation period, should go through all the steps of ages of evolution; he begins as a tadpole, then a fish and so on until millions of years of progress is compressed into a period of nine months. But one thing never changes; he still falls for that old badger game. Beaned on the head with an apple, a sly glance, a glimpse of a shapely leg as she climbs the tree, the pursuit, the capture, the steadying influence of that leg hooked over a limb; delusions of mastery, children, mortgages, swimming pools, taxes and all the rest of the things that go to make up our civilization. We fondly think that we have made progress from that first eventful day in Nod, but we have done so only in ways that make the woman's life less strenuous and more exciting. Man himself can never hope to improve upon his own lot. He is still a frustrated though shaven ape, charging about the earth trying to evade the curse of Cain and to secure forgetfulness and peace of mind; yet he vents his lust for retail or wholesale murder upon his fellows and prays in public for peace on earth, good will to men.

If that Nod maiden had just let well enough alone and stayed up in that tree, what a peaceful world this would have been. But no; like her daughters of today, she took the risk of

Taken from Life with Women and How to Survive it
by Joseph H. Peck, Prentice Hall, 1961.

To My Husband

When I was eight & nine & ten,
my stepfather slung me across
him in bed, his alien erection rising
hard into my doughy thigh.
He lifted the flap of my rose-
bud panties when I was eleven.
I still have those panties, bunched
at the bottom of a lingerie bag, proof.
A lifetime of nightmares about
        jacking him off or
            him murdering my boyfriends or
                me laughing as he straddles my chest
                      and beats me.
I'll never forget,
never recover anything.
I'll wear them for you if you want.

Selfish

My little brother pissed
        himself every night last week.
He's seven years old,
potty trained at three.
He's back in diapers, though,
        but only at night, only at home.
He relies on second-grade mercy
        when he soils himself at school,
        tries to hide in the corner
        of the library.

His name is Edward.
When I saw him two days before Christmas
he could suddenly read. I never saw
him sitting at the kitchen table, wrangling
his Rs or trapping his Ts, but when I gave
him a GameBoy he showed me by reading
the entire Pokemon intro scene. He's missing
his two front teeth.
        When he was born
I took the first tear rolling down his cheek
and put it in my mouth.

I thought it would make him a part of me.
A permanent savior. The biggest big sister
whom he could only call "Bit-nee" when he was three.

I've only seen him twice since last year.

It all leads back
to what his father did to me;

the betrayal of our mother demands
another name I don't know how to say.

What I do know is that in every cell swims
a piece of my brother, and we share
50% of the same DNA—

but the man who fucked my mother to father
him fucked me the same way.

What do I get to say when our mother
knows all and remarried him anyway?

As an adult I can claim
that I will never speak
to her or him again

but what that means is I can't see
Edward, today or any day. I saw
him before Christmas by sneaking
in when the parents were away.

CPS didn't investigate
because it wasn't a "first-hand
knowledgeable claim."
I never saw Edward wet
his pants in the grocery store, small
hands pinching his wet crotch
as he whimpered
"Oh man oh man oh man"

I was just told.
I'm not close enough to see
where his father's hands do
or do not go.

I swear
to god I want to save him.
        But for some
lie that lives inside
my mind I cannot raise my cry
for his small,
gap-toothed smile.

My baby brother pissed himself
        every night last week while
I slept between clean sheets
labelled "selfish" and "free."

The Goldfish

I wanted to win goldfish at the school carnival,
little lives,
miniscule gold flakes up-ended

in a globe
cinched tight, stale water & air only inches
below the dartboard.

The primal thrill of a life for a prize.
But I wasn't allowed
to play—stepfather growling stories

of fish being sealed
up so long they sputter out
dead upon release.

Only stepfather could provide life.

Ten years later he'd convince me to buy a pair
of teardrop goldfish,
a surprise for my high school boyfriend, to prove

he couldn't keep
anything alive. "See?" stepfather says
when they suffocate.

Dissonance

> *"I myself am hell;*
> *nobody's here—"*
> —Robert Lowell, "Skunk Hour"

My husband read my journal and bled,
a deep maroon bloom on white tissue.
It's been two weeks since my journal fell open
Yet when we climb into bed his nose bleeds.

Deep maroon blooms on white chest tissue—
Another man grabbed me by the negligee.
When my husband climbs into bed his nose bleeds,
Thinking of lace fisted in a bunch between my breasts—

Another man grabbed me by the negligee.
Nighttime drags us under:
Lace frothing between my breasts,
He plunged my vows til I popped his head.

Nighttime drags us under even though
My husband won't kiss me again—
(even when I pop their heads)
I never cum away from home.

My husband won't kiss me again
(We're all adulterers now)
(I never came away from home)
Dreams of drowning me instead.

My husband dreams of drowning me.
Two weeks ago he picked up my journal.
We're all adulterers now.
My husband read my journal and bled.

Deboned

I miss
the thunder of his hipbone
need, rolling me flat
against the feathers of morning, the crawl
of his jaw down
white belly and up
wet throat—hooked
hands I long
to hang on (we married
our sex away)

I'll turn
down black sheets
with my teeth, lick
cum-stains clean with
tongue, on my knees,
naked
and gagged
tight with nylon need
(no one spanks me)

I'll pinch
myself for you, dis-
embodied lover—
spit my pink—

if I dress in honeymoon blue,
will you crack me over your knee?

Exposition

Before my stepfather came
in the front door, paid me in dimes to bend
before him, polish his brown leather shoes—

there was a storybook between my legs I knew
only a boy could read. I pulled one in
the closet of the playroom and asked him to see, to lick
each one of my six-year-old teeth, his tongue a metal shock
like a fat copper fish. I pulled the little boy over me like
a sun, like a god, made him lash me with rope
to the swing set pole, years before

my stepfather asked my hungry
mother to dance. I already knew
about the room
inside me when
his heart throbbed
against the zipper's leash.

Transatlantic Relapse

I, sober 22 days after drinking Listerine
in my blistering husband's face when I had 126 days clean,
order a whiskey. Then a red. I wasted
me, my open fist dripping
grit.
This is who I am, Brave Woman Who Flies
to Europe Alone. But I am also a wife made heavy
with whiskey stones, clunking inside
my soggy sack of bones.
I hurl into the white blind of morning.

Stepfather as Wolf

When he prowled into the yard, flattened
the baby's breath, the mother was fed up with kneading
dough to live. A daughter to raise
was a body too many—she never asked
to be a widow, to sleep with a baby instead of a man,
to watch a girl full of yeast rise as her own breasts gave
to crumbs in her own hands.

The mother flung door and apron wide
for his thick animal scent. With his teeth inside
her, she forgot she was a mother, became only flesh,
young between his molars, the entree instead of the dead
baker's wife. At night she'd rub Wolf's furred shoulders as he slept
on her good goose pillows, run her fingers from the base
of his snout to the wiry tip of his tail.

Inside his mouth she forgave
the bruises on her daughter's thigh, the spot
behind her daughter's ear that each morning glistened
with canine spit:

if her child hid the fresh bread of her body in thick red cloaks
if his breath reeked of young meat
if he chewed her fast enough

the mother's mind went flour-white: spat.

To My Husband

I don't keep.

When you trembled inside
your high school girlfriend, junker car parked
at the canyon's slit, my best guess

is I was drugged between my parent's
orange sheets—he used
to do that, palm me sedatives whenever I began
to shriek. Pills were better than memory,
better than love, especially his. I split

from my mind that day,
inner thighs slick with loss
of feeling.

Inscape

Years deep, my husband watches me
shoot vodka straight, spew
pools of vomit and gaping sky.

I ask his body to fill the rest.
I tell the therapist there are potholes
in my chest, caves where my fathers drilled.

She puts a vibrating node in each palm, plugs
me to a hypnotic machine purring
left… right… left… right…

a naked child grinds herself to chalk
against my ribcage, rattling
gravel in her lungs. She needs

to know he didn't mean to hurt
her, not really, he knows girls
made of stone don't bleed.

Three Little Sisters

The three little pigs were daughters
whose mother ran out of slop.
She gave them each other, crawled
into the wolf, and died.

The first pig sister found grass and smoked
her ham away. She married first chance
and let her animal brain cool
in the TV's blue glare, all memory of canines
and family buzzing to gray.

The second pig sister quit food forever, frosted
her hungry bones in floral print and fake lashes.
She hated her hide and the chops men would gnaw.
If she played the farmer's games right,
she could suck instead of squeal at night.

The third pig sister did everything right.
She got perfect grades, a second degree,
took all her meds, took her walks outside
til she skipped off a cliff in bright sunlight.
The note on the counter said she was fine.

To My Husband

Your socks lay bunched
like dead rats on the floor:
I won't clean up anymore.
I have named my fear of men and quit
feeling for you all.

I see the scars on my ribcage
(where I asked you to sign)
as initials from the colonizers,
carving their love into my bark-white skin.

I am twenty-four and realize I've been
giving my life to the brutest bidder since
my stepfather fucked my childhood away.
If I married a man like my Daddy and got

him to mark me, I could win.
In the dark, I thought you were him.

**After Watching the Performance Poem,
"We Keep Our Victims Ready"**

Karen Finley coated her naked
chest in Double Dark Chocolate Cake on stage,
rubbed crumbs into her collarbone and cleavage
to the audience's drooling roar. In nothing
but red panties and bandana she laughed,
feeding them the dessert of her body,
her sugar-coated breath.
It's a strip-tease, a strip-search of all the bulges
in their minds when a body comes before them as feed.
When she takes the mic between

her teeth she is the sweetest thing they've ever seen.
But when she opens her mouth,

the men with their drool will rage until the NEA takes
her grant away. When what appears to be a comic treat
turns into a shrieking speech on daddies who get fat
on incest, the dudes in the room will bitch til Karen's right
to free speech is overruled by the Supreme—our government
likes women sweet, not "indecent" or "obscene." If she screams

"Sure, I've had my share of love letters too"
but doesn't stop at
*"All those scars on your body baby is evidence
of my fucking love for you evidence of my fucking
fucking love for you"*
they'll run her out of her life baby: I yell at the screen

the daddies don't want to hear it and they'll scar
you, the men in the room will take your voice
for their brothers outside

who smeared their feces on fifteen-year-old Tawana Brawley's
face, their brothers who raped the girl you covered
yourself in chocolate to imitate, they stuffed
Tawana in a garbage sack and they'll sack you too

for every award you've got because
half the men playing fingerpaint with shit are the law
and you can't fight the law baby
they'll cut your pussy with steak knives
and drizzle mole on your mouth because Tawana is black
and you've both got cunts so they'll win win win

Tawana is gone and your father shot
himself in the garage because he loved you
all the crumbs on your tits baby are evidence
of his fucking fucking love for you

baby I've eaten chocolate cake too
but if you don't stop at
"I want you to get the fuck out of my life"
the men who are your father who are the law
the men they'll fuck your skull
and smash the plate.

Does My Brother Dream of Showers?

My sister is my brother now. Out
of the stuffed rabbit's hide, he pulls
a flashlight, a marker, a knife,

arterial threads dangling.
I am drunk; think about
when he was she and she was eight years old.

At a Build-a-Bear outside Salt Lake,
my little sister picked the rabbit's limp
hide, little pelt on a hook. Together we filled

it with white stuffing; my sister kissed
her wishes into a tiny red heart, slipped
it inside before running fat thread up

the rabbit's backside.
I am 24 and not blacked out yet;
my sister is my brother now and he is now 14.

He brings the rabbit to our sleepover, matted
with age and love and drool. My brother wears
a girdle to keep the budding breasts in; when I was

14, I also hid my body inside XL hoodies, boot-cut
jeans. When I pass out, I dream of my brother's
father following me into the shower again.

There is a red pocketknife where the little
rabbit heart used to be.

Too awake

I can feel
it—full
of blood, his need, slumming
behind my hipbone
on Saturday morning.
When I don't open he takes
himself in one hand, unzips
his phone with the other.

This marriage is my fault. Past me,
men have come to mow
the lawn, a backdrop of blades.
My dog howls at the door.

Domesticated

Because the flavor of love is eggs, I let the dog lick my plate. Each morning he pads ahead expectantly, watches me slosh out of bed and close the door behind us so my husband can sleep. I fill the dog bowl before I heat the stove, break a couple eggs, slit each yellow breast with a wooden spatula. He'll gorge and then sit on my toes, eyes trained on each turn of my wrist. How bland it would be, wolfing and shitting the same brown mush twice a day. It's such a bloodless feeding—no sacrifice at all, no shattering on the pan's edge, milky flesh sizzling on low. After lapping my leftovers the dog yips for water; the salt of it overwhelms his soft palate. If he ever tasted blood it was raw hamburger, loveless on the kitchen floor. He never killed anything. In a lifetime, the only bloody egg I've seen I threw away, made my husband start fresh while I left the room. He'll wake after I leave, reheat the coffee and plop in front of the TV. Once upon a time he cooked eggs every day, over-easy in bacon grease. The dog's chin matted with gold.

Mastectomy

Men stopped sleeping with my grand-
Mother after the surgeon took
Her left breast: at thirty-three
She hid the puckered frown of bare

Chest beneath padded bras where once
My grandfather, my uncle, and
My father sucked. At night
I nurse my husband now,

Even as my grandmother closes
Her eyes, gives thanks to the knife.

January

In summer
and early fall I ran
this trail. Once
I raced home with
a berry in my fist
for you, a small
heart lolling
in my palm.
You taught me
the universe tastes
like raspberries.
Today there is
nothing blooming
over a backyard fence:
the world
sealed
in snow.
In the canal's belly
beneath the woolen
rosehips lives
a speechless splash
of green, watercress clustered
like sisters in the water.
I take
a picture, think
for a quote about hope
to send you
and interrupt your
metal indoor day,
the war on the radio
and in your brain.
I will turn the ashes into snowflakes
where I can.

Alaska

All I want to do is write that mother
Fucker out of my chest,
Every dark hair, each manipulative daydream.
I want to scrub his genes out of my siblings
With Listerine and spirit them away,
Take new names from constellations and jump
Onto trains, head north, fly away, bathe
With ice chips til we're numb. I'll teach

Them to (un)lock their screaming
And how many murders end domestic disputes.
We'll write a new story, one where we bloom
As triplets from a grizzly bear's womb, our mother
A mountain. There will be no fathers

For us, only love, only streams
Of bright summer fish, midnights laced
With gold ribbon. The mountain
Will hold us to her earthen breast, all warm
Breath, three bears bumping noses through
The night. Safe.

Britt Allen takes revenge on the circumstances of her life by being blunt, bare, and brave on the page. She contends with a male-dominated society and abusive childhood as she moves into adulthood and the supposed saving grace of a marriage. Her speaker confesses traumatic memories, marital betrayals, and harmful coping mechanisms in a lyrical way, adding her voice to the abused poets of past and present who have also asked themselves—*how can a raped daughter grow up to love a man?* To break the silence forced upon her by an abusive parent, the speaker examines the pattern of sexual failures in her life, as well as her roles as a female, daughter, sister, and wife through poetry. Follow her work at brittallen.org.

www.ingramcontent.com/pod-product-compliance
Lightning Source LLC
LaVergne TN
LVHW041522070426
835507LV00012B/1749